JONATHAN

THE FAITHFUL FRIEND

TOLD BY CARINE MACKEN[...]
ILLUSTRATIONS BY FRED [...]

Copyright © 2007 Carine Mackenzie
Published by Christian Focus Publications, Geanies House,
Fearn, Tain, Ross-shire, IV20 1TW, Scotland, U.K.
Printed in China.
ISBN: 978-1-84550-289-8
www.christianfocus.com

CF4•K
Because you're never
too young to know Jesus

Jonathan was the eldest son of King Saul, who was the first king of Israel. Saul was a tall, handsome man and a mighty warrior.

Jonathan was a brave soldier too – a commander in the
army fighting against the Philistines.

As eldest son, Jonathan was the crown prince, heir to the throne of Israel.

But Saul his father became more and more disobedient to God's laws.

Samuel, God's prophet, took a message to Saul from God. "You have been foolish. You have not kept the commandments of God. Your kingdom will not continue. Another man will be king after you, not your son."

God had chosen David to be the next king and so sent Samuel to his home to anoint him with oil.

When Saul was depressed or troubled he would send for David to play the harp to cheer him.

David did many wonderful and brave deeds. He was clever and popular. Saul grew jealous of David. He realised that David had been anointed to be the next king of Israel. The people sang songs about David and his great deeds on the battlefield.

Jonathan was not jealous. He was a faithful friend to David.

Jonathan and David made a covenant (or special agreement) to seal their friendship. Jonathan gave his cloak and his armour and belt to David. He did this to show that he knew that God had chosen David as king.

Saul became so jealous that he even tried to kill David with a spear. David behaved wisely at this time because God was with him.

Saul told his son Jonathan, "David should be killed." But godly Jonathan was a true friend to David. He warned him of his father's wicked plan. "Be on your guard," he said. "Hide until the morning. I will speak to my father and tell you everything tomorrow."

Jonathan spoke well about David to his father. He reminded him of all the great deeds David had done for his king and country.

"Why would you kill David without a just cause?" he asked.

Saul relented. Jonathan told David that it was safe to return to the king's house.

Before long Saul became jealous again. David was called to play music to try to soothe him. King Saul grabbed a spear and tried to pin David to the wall. David managed to escape that night.

Saul kept on hunting David but David fled from his home.

He went to tell Samuel the prophet all that Saul had done.

Jonathan was still a faithful friend. "My father will tell me what he is planning," Jonathan said. "I will do all I can to help you."

David and Jonathan renewed their vows of friendship and made a plan. David was afraid to go near King Saul. He was sure he wanted to kill him.

"You hide in the field," Jonathan told David. "I will find out how my father is feeling."

They decided on a special signal.

Saul held a special feast in his house, but David's place was empty.

Saul thought there might be a good reason for his absence but when David was missing the next day, he began to be suspicious.

"Why has David not come to the feast yesterday or today?" he asked Jonathan.

Jonathan made an excuse for David. "He asked permission to go and see his family in Bethlehem."

Saul became very angry with Jonathan.

"I know you have chosen David as a friend, but do you not realise that you will not be king because of him? He should be killed."

"Why should he be killed? What has he done?" retorted Jonathan.

Saul became so angry he threw a spear at Jonathan, trying to kill him.

Jonathan realised that Saul definitely intended to kill David.

Jonathan was so angry with Saul, his father, that he got up from the table without eating the meal.

Jonathan had to warn David as arranged. In the morning he went out to the field with a little servant boy. David was hiding nearby.

"Run and find the arrows that I shoot," he told the boy.

Jonathan shot an arrow. As the boy ran to fetch it, Jonathan shouted out, "Is not the arrow beyond you?" That was the pre-arranged signal that it was not safe for David to return.

"Make haste, hurry, do not delay!" shouted Jonathan, loudly enough for David to hear.

The little boy knew nothing of the secret plan and picked up the arrows and hurried back to his master Jonathan.

As the boy returned to the city with the weapons, David appeared from his hiding place.

Jonathan and David wept. "Go in peace," Jonathan said to David. "We have made a vow to each other in the name of the Lord. May the Lord be in the relationship between you and me, and between our children and our descendants in years to come."

Jonathan and David showed true godly love to each other. God commands us to have this love for others. "Love your neighbour as yourself," God tells us.

David hurried off, fleeing from danger. Jonathan went back to the city. Saul kept on hunting for David but God kept David safe.

One day Jonathan met David in a forest. He encouraged David and reminded him of God's promise to him, assuring him that God would make him the new king of Israel. "Even my father Saul knows that."

Again David and Jonathan made a covenant before the Lord. It would be their last meeting.

David stayed in the woods and Jonathan went back to his own house.

The Philistines fought against Saul and his sons and the men of Israel.

At Mount Gilboa, the battle became so fierce that Jonathan and two of his brothers were killed. Saul was severely wounded. He died there too, by falling on his own sword.

When word came to David of the deaths of Saul and his sons, he was very sad. He composed a special song of lamentation about Saul and Jonathan, which was to be taught to all the people of Judah.

David then journeyed to Hebron where the men of Judah anointed him as king.

There was war between the house of David and Saul's descendants for several years. Some time later David was anointed as king over all the tribes of Israel as God had promised years before. David was thirty years old when he was made king and he reigned for forty years.

One day King David asked, "Is there anyone left of the family of Saul? I would like to show him kindness for my friend Jonathan's sake."

Ziba, Saul's servant, told him about Jonathan's son Mephibosheth.

When news came about the deaths of Jonathan and Saul, Mephibosheth's nurse fled with him from danger. However, the little boy fell and was badly injured. As a result he was lame.

David called Mephibosheth to his house.

"Don't be afraid," he said. "I want to show you kindness for your father Jonathan's sake."

David gave Mephibosheth the land that had once belonged to Saul. Mephibosheth would always be welcome to eat at King David's table.

Mephibosheth was unable to work the land himself so Ziba and his sons worked for him. David showed Mephibosheth great kindness.

Jonathan truly loved the Lord God with all his heart, soul and mind. He loved David as a true friend and was not jealous when God chose David to be king. He was loyal to his father Saul too, although he realised his weakness.

God helped Jonathan to live righteously.

Pray that you will be like Jonathan and love God with all your heart, soul and mind. We love God because he first loved us and gave his Son to die for us on the cross. Jesus is the best friend that you can have.